Thirty

A Collection of Personal Quotes, Advice, and Lessons

By

Emily Maroutian

ISBN-13: 978-1506116617

First Printing

Printed and bound in the United States of America by Createspace, a division of Amazon.com

MAROUTIAN
E N T E R T A I N M E N T
Los Angeles, California
www.maroutian.com

#1 – Quote

What people think about you has more to do with their habitual thinking than with who you really are. You, as you are right now, are filtered through decades of their life experiences, traumas, disappointments, heartaches, and suffering. It is a reflection of their patterns of thought and stories about life. Their judgment has nothing to do with you as a whole because the experience of you cannot be separated from their experience of life.

-Emily Maroutian

#2 – Advice

Nothing from the past can still exist unless we drag it into the present moment through our minds. Holding onto past pain creates present pain. Holding onto old fears creates new fears. Holding onto former injuries caused by others is an act of current self-injury. What's done is gone. The only way it can live within us again is through our willingness to revive it in this moment.

-Emily Maroutian

#3 – Lesson

The people around you are either enhancers of your dream or distracters from it. Some fill you up through support, love, and inspiration and others empty you with drama, draining conversations, and emotional manipulation. You will know by the way you feel after every interaction. Your likelihood for success depends just as greatly on who you spend time with as much as how much you work on it. Your work will become harder and more challenging with more distracters. Surround yourself with enhancers and your work will feel easier and lighter.

-Emily Maroutian

#4 – Quote

Resilience is choosing the hopeful thought over the resigning thought day after day, regardless of what happens.

-Emily Maroutian

#5 – Advice

If you want to know where to find your contribution to the world, look at your wounds. When you learn how to heal them, teach others.

-Emily Maroutian

#6 – Lesson

Words are things. They are real. They are alive. They have a smell, a sound, a taste, a touch, they can be seen, and they can be felt. Even if it's all in the mind. You can see the word "tree," you can taste the word "watermelon," you can smell the word "jasmine," you can feel the pain of the word "fire," you can hear the word "guitar." They elicit a powerful response from the person receiving it. They have the ability to move us into action, anger us, make us fall in love, express passion, express sadness, wage war, create peace. They color our world. They bring us to life. Their power lies in how they are used.

-Emily Maroutian

#7 – Quote

Pain might make you stronger or smarter for the next time around, but learning to heal that pain makes you wiser for the rest of your life.

-Emily Maroutian

#8 – Advice

Each soul is equipped with its own GPS. If you follow someone else's, you'll get lost. They'll arrive at their destination full of joy, but you'll arrive at their destination full of emptiness and frustration. Follow your own instincts; they will never get you lost.

-Emily Maroutian

#9 – Lesson

You can't criticize yourself into self-love. Whatever change
that is inspired by self-criticism will be criticized later as well.
It's the critical and self-hating mindset that requires the
change—not anything else in the body or character.

-Emily Maroutian

#10 – Quote

The difference between a soulmate and a cellmate is your freedom. Stuckness is not stability. Possession is not love. Control is not caring.

-Emily Maroutian

#11 – Advice

The problem with thinking you're too sensitive is that you're saying you're not justified in your feelings. You dismiss your right to feel whatever it is that you feel. You immediately invalidate yourself because you are "too" sensitive and shouldn't be feeling what you're feeling.

If you continuously invalidate your feelings, then you will stop trusting your instincts. You will stop trusting your internal GPS and you will wander all over the place. That's when you'll begin to make mistake after mistake in relationships, in career, always making off moves and then shaming yourself afterwards for not knowing better. If you judge your emotions, you won't be able to trust them. If you can't trust them, you can't navigate through life accurately.

-Emily Maroutian

#12 – Lesson

Haters hate because there's something missing within them or within their lives that they see in you. They believe they can't have it, and that causes negative emotion within them. If they believed they could have it too, they would be inspired by you to get it themselves. It would be a positive emotion. The fact that it brings out hate or jealousy is because they don't believe they can. Belief in possibility is the difference between jealousy and inspiration.

-Emily Maroutian

#13 – Quote

Stress is when you hold two opposing thoughts in your mind about the same subject. "I want to do it, but I can't do it." "I want that, but I can't have that." "I'm sitting in traffic, but I shouldn't be." All stressful emotions that arise are the result of an opposing thought that contradicts a desire.

-Emily Maroutian

#14 – Advice

When someone tells you something about another person, don't take it as a fact. Everyone experiences their current life and the people they encounter through their past experiences, expectations, and life stories. Just because someone has had a hard time with someone else, doesn't mean you will too. Just because it was someone else's experience of that person, doesn't mean it will be yours. But if you believe what they say, then it will be.

-Emily Maroutian

#15 – Lesson

You have to value your time, energy, and love before you can offer it to anyone else as something worthwhile.

-Emily Maroutian

#16 – Quote

Insecure people use whatever strength they have to keep others down so they can feel good about themselves. Confident people lift others up *because* they feel good about themselves.

-Emily Maroutian

#17 – Advice

If you dilute yourself trying to please everyone, you won't
have anything substantial or powerful to offer anyone,
including yourself. Be selective in how you spend your energy;
it is your life's currency.

-Emily Maroutian

#18 – Lesson

If you feel defensive about something, it inspires others to attack it. The more resistance you put up toward a subject, the more others will push back. Defense signals to an offense that you are ready for a fight.

-Emily Maroutian

#19 – Quote

Resistance isn't there to stop you from getting what you want;
it's there to strengthen you into the person who can handle it.

-Emily Maroutian

#20 – Advice

View all past events in kind-sight. You made it through. You are better now, wiser, and stronger. Of course you're going to wonder what you were thinking back then. You have grown now. It's that growth that makes you want to judge your past. It's because you have a wiser and more mature pair of eyes now. But resist the urge to be unkind to yourself. You don't reprimand yourself for when you were two years old and just learning to walk. You don't sit and think about all the times you fell down as you were trying to balance yourself. Well, that's what you were doing at sixteen as well, and at thirty-six and even seventy-six. You were just learning balance.

-Emily Maroutian

#21 – Lesson

Sometimes we need time to grieve for a future that might have been. After a loss of a relationship, friendship, job, or even the loss of the possibility of those things can be a painful process. When a possibility is cancelled out, it can feel like a sort of loss, even if we didn't really lose anything. Even if we didn't have it to begin with. Just knowing something can't happen can be very painful. It can create a state of mourning within us. However, the sooner we let go of that possibility, another one will become open to us. There is no real loss in the universe, just pieces moving toward each other and shifting away from each other. Where there is one, there is another.

-Emily Maroutian

#22 – Quote

The lacks we experienced as adolescents become the driving forces within us as adults. We are pulled to create what we didn't have or didn't get to experience. And so we become the adults we needed as children.

-Emily Maroutian

#23 – Advice

Every single form of progress has been made by someone who noticed that something could be lighter, faster, easier, or better. It's okay to notice which areas in your life require progress, but that's not the same energy as complaining. One leaves you open to change while the other keeps you stuck in what you don't like. Notice the contrast, but instead of continuously commenting on it, relax and allow the solution to come to you.

-Emily Maroutian

#24 – Lesson

Joyful people will never intentionally hurt others. They have to be in a lower emotional state to justify that kind of behavior. The best way we can change a violent world is to encourage people to follow their joy and to not judge how they pursue it.

-Emily Maroutian

#25 – Quote

If you enter into a conversation or argument with someone
you love with the intention of "winning," then you are really
fighting a battle. You are trying to take your opponent down
or put them in their place. The only thing you are going to
win is a broken relationship. Winning over your partner
means your whole relationship is losing. The only time anyone
wins in an argument is if both parties leave it feeling heard,
respected, and loved.

-Emily Maroutian

#26 – Advice

Your life is an advertisement for your beliefs. You can never force it on anyone who isn't interested. If they want what you have, they will come to you. Let your life be the evidence; let it speak for you.

-Emily Maroutian

#27 – Lesson

A story is merely a relative narrowing of perception. The villain of one story is the hero of another. And so the enemy you believe is trying to take you down is really the lead of another story trying to overcome an obstacle. Everyone is the main character of their own story, the central figure just trying to find some kind of happiness or peace.

-Emily Maroutian

#28 – Quote

If you choose from a place of loneliness or desperation, you'll soon find yourself in the same place yet again. Impatience and rushing are symptoms of a worrisome mind and low self-worth. Nothing worthwhile is ever built on the foundation of desperation.

-Emily Maroutian

#29 – Advice

Too often we look at ourselves through the eyes of future possibility and then blame or shame ourselves for not becoming it. You are you, now, in this very moment, and there is nothing wrong with or missing from it. Yes, there are many things you didn't become, but look at all you are. Look at all you've been through. Don't let the possibility of something else, somewhere else, in some other time ruin your life now. Now is all you'll ever have. Ease into the moment and accept what you are. Your life will blossom when you do.

-Emily Maroutian

#30 – Lesson

When you trek up the mountain, your legs become stronger
for next time. Each subsequent climb toughens you up.
Exposure to hard experiences makes life easier in the long
run.

-Emily Maroutian

#31 – Quote

The difference between a boss and a leader is that a boss will order you around to fulfill his plan, but a leader will inspire you into his vision. Leaders will tie their vision with your own so well that every action you take will feel like you are working toward your own goal. They will show you that your vision and their vision are really one in the same. Then, you're not working FOR them. You're working with them—on something you both believe in.

-Emily Maroutian

#32 – Advice

Wherever you're going, whatever you're doing, just remember it's you who has to walk those miles; it's you who has to take those actions. It's beneficial to listen to other people's advice, but never forget it's your life; you are the one who has to live it every second of every day.

-Emily Maroutian

#33 – Lesson

The only insults that hurt are the ones we agree with on some level. People will say many things to us, some of which might make us angry because they're not true, but the only words that hurt are those we've said to ourselves. So when we hear them from the outside world, they sting because we think they validate the unwanted belief.

-Emily Maroutian

#34 – Quote

Nature grows through breaking things down, through cracking things open, through opening up, spilling out, and then blossoming. Growth can feel like a destructive process. That's because it is. You have to crack open your old self for new aspects to bloom.

-Emily Maroutian

#35 – Advice

If you don't use resistance against resistance, it will turn into
ease and then flow right through you. It's the pushing back
that causes struggle and makes things harder. Negative
emotion feeds off of your resistance to it. You either have to
let it pass or step into another flow.

-Emily Maroutian

#36 – Lesson

The more you try to avoid something, the more you create it. There is no such thing as avoidance in energy because the energy is focused on the fear, not the desire. This is why we create things we don't want and can't understand how we did it. It's usually because we took actions to avoid something we feared instead of taking actions to create the thing we desire.

-Emily Maroutian

#37 – Quote

I am not here for your understanding of who I am. I am here for your understanding of who you are. I am your mirror. How you feel about me, what you see in me, the thoughts that arise from your encounter of me, the judgments you hold about me, are all reflections of you. They have nothing to do with me.

-Emily Maroutian

#38 – Advice

Energy is the currency of the universe. When you "pay" attention to something, you buy that experience. So when you allow your consciousness to focus on someone or something that annoys you, you feed it your energy, and it reciprocates with the experience of being annoyed. Be selective in your focus because your attention feeds the energy of it and keeps it alive, not just within you, but in the collective consciousness as well.

-Emily Maroutian

#39 – Lesson

Instinct will always lead you to the best possible outcome that is available in this moment. We don't need a why when instinct is involved because it's the feeling pathway to our highest good. Whether it's run, sign the deal, don't trust him, marry her, or wait to have children, our instincts come from a deeper knowing that shouldn't be rationalized away. We rarely ever regret following our instincts, but we almost always regret not listening to them.

-Emily Maroutian

#40 – Quote

Too often, we use feelings as excuses for bad behavior. We say we acted out of character because we were angry or upset. If that's the case, then we are not acting out of character. It is very much a part of our character; it just took intense emotion to bring it out to the surface. But it was still in us to begin with. We are responsible for how we behave, always. Triggers don't mean anything if there isn't anything there to trigger.

-Emily Maroutian

#41 – Advice

When we pray at the dinner table, we infuse the food in front of us with the energy of appreciation. This is why we hold hands and encircle the food with love and appreciation. But when we debate politics or argue with each other at the dinner table, we infuse the food with the energy of our anger and hatred. Always remember to speak well around food; what you put into them will be placed back into you.

-Emily Maroutian

#42 – Lesson

When you seek to cage a partner because you don't trust them, it's really because you yourself exist in a cage as well and are seeking comfort in a cellmate. It can come in the form of any kind of insecurity about the self. There is some part of yourself you don't trust, or dislike and wish lock away. It could be because you don't feel attractive enough, because you feel you can't express yourself, can't live out your dreams, or anything else restrictive. Only self-restricted people want to restrict others. When you free yourself from your own limits and restrictions, you will only seek out others who are free as well. Then, trust will not even be an issue.

-Emily Maroutian

#43 – Quote

You are a conscious energy vibration manifested in an organic
body in this current time-space reality. A droplet of god
specifically focused in this moment of eternity. Perhaps that
shows up as a writer, a doctor, a mother, or any other label,
but underneath those things you are the universe in a
condensed form.

-Emily Maroutian

#44 – Advice

Don't take on other people's feelings just because they are available to you. Getting angry with an angry person never calms them down, and getting sad with a sad person never cheers them up. You have to stand firmly in your joy or peace so that others can rise to your feelings instead of you lowering to theirs.

-Emily Maroutian

#45 – Lesson

When we're mad or upset at someone, we refuse to think good thoughts about them. We find it hard to say nice things, almost as if they don't deserve our good words. But those thoughts and words come from within us and dominate the way *we* feel. What happens takes place within us, and we deserve good thoughts whether it's about us or someone else.

-Emily Maroutian

#46 – Quote

Hate that feels justified is not any less damaging than hate that can't be justified. The feeling creates the same energy regardless of whether we can justify it in our minds.

-Emily Maroutian

#47 – Advice

If you train people to always expect sacrifice from you, you'll upset them when you begin to say no. Say no anyway. If they believe the task is important, they'll find someone else to do it or they'll do it themselves. If they don't believe it's important enough to find other ways, then you shouldn't be doing it at all. Your time and energy is just as important as theirs and much more important than a task that can be easily dropped. The important tasks will get done whether you do it, they do it themselves, or they find someone else to do it. The non-important tasks will drop away. When you value your time and energy, others won't ask you to waste it on frivolous tasks they can do themselves.

-Emily Maroutian

#48 – Lesson

Whatever greatness you recognize in another is a reflection of your own potential greatness. If you can see it, appreciate it, or have respect for it, you can activate it within yourself. In the same way, whatever you find repulsive in another you end up re-pulsing into your character. You infuse, you electrify, you bring to life that characteristic, and it pulsates again within you. If you judge it, condemn it, or hate it, you bring it to life and become a part of it.

-Emily Maroutian

#49 – Quote

What no one tells you about "waking up" is that when you do,
so do the demons in you who have been asleep for a while.
Everything wakes up: your consciousness, your sleeping fears,
old traumas and wounds. All of it begins to stir inside until
you can consciously heal it or give it some peace.

-Emily Maroutian

#50 – Advice

If something is bothering you, stop thinking about it. It may seem counter-productive, but struggle rarely yields the right answers. The word on the tip of your tongue always comes when you stop forcing it by moving on to something else. The quality of the answer that comes from struggle is very different than the quality of the answer that comes from ease.

-Emily Maroutian

#51 – Lesson

One day you will believe that relationships don't last and you will want to use it as an excuse not to get close to other people. Life is about the experience, not the outcome. Life is not win or lose. Life is win *and* lose. It's about living it all. It's about the love you made between the start and the end. It's about the joys, the growth, and the laughter. Life is about living, period. Yes, living things have endings, but that fact shouldn't stop you from actually living.

-Emily Maroutian

#52 – Quote

If we stopped teaching cultural and familial suffering to just one generation, we would greatly change the trajectory of the world. All wars, battles, injustice, and acts of terrorism are created through teaching youth that someone else is responsible for our pain and subsequently needs to be punished.

-Emily Maroutian

#53 – Advice

Don't spend your energy trying to get people to like your energy. That makes it forceful and therefore unlikable. It's a catch-22. Instead, you have to become easy with it. Let it flow out naturally; that makes similar energies gravitate toward you. It won't be forced or aggressive, and they will naturally like it because it's similar to theirs.

-Emily Maroutian

#54 – Lesson

Whatever characteristic we think we lack within ourselves we will find attractive in a mate. Most attraction is an attempt to possess a trait we believe we don't or can't have. "He's so charming," might be an admission that we wish to have his ability to get what he wants through charm. "She is very smart," might be an admission that we wish to have her ability to use intelligence to create something valuable in life. Whatever we value in our mate is in part an admission to what we feel we lack within ourselves. All human beings are attracted to the idea of being whole. Most think they need others to complete themselves and so they try to obtain their missing traits by being with the people who possess them.

-Emily Maroutian

#55 – Quote

There's no such thing as going back. Once you've grown and expanded from the lessons and experiences, you can never go back to your original form. You can return to someone again, but neither of you will be the same as before.

-Emily Maroutian

#56 – Advice

Stop trying. Stop struggling. Stop forcing. Who you are doesn't take energy or effort. It is the easiest thing to be. If it's not easy, it's not really you. It's a dream of someone you want to be because you think it's better than who you really are. Most likely, you picked it up from watching others being that naturally. What you're seeking isn't the thing in the other person that you're mimicking; it's the ease in which that person behaves, the confidence in which they flow, the naturalness of their being, the comfort in who they are. What you really want to is feel good about who you are. That's all. You don't want to be them—you want to feel good about being you.

-Emily Maroutian

#57 – Lesson

Any human characteristic one person finds repulsive, another might find attractive. So who fixes what? One person's arrogance is another person's strong will. One person's bitch is another person's leadership. Something that might be viewed as selfishness might be someone finally giving up decades of people-pleasing and choosing to put themselves first.

We also don't know the reasons why people took on those characteristics and what they had to adopt to survive. Those things are survival mechanisms and are deep rooted in pain. So if we give up the need to "fix" those things in other people and we choose to love them anyway, those things become transformed. We're not saying there's something wrong with you and you must fix it; making others wrong doesn't heal them. We're saying, I love you even though you are hurt. Love is healing.

-Emily Maroutian

#58 – Quote

In the beginning stages of self-development, it's normal to
isolate yourself from others and work on yourself. After a
while, you have to start building those social bonds again
because it's in other people that you will see whether you've
succeeded in your efforts. They will be the mirrors to what's
happening inside you. Are you still easily angered or
frustrated, are you still judgmental of others? Then you need
more work. People are our teachers. Anyone can be at peace
by themselves. Anyone can be their true selves alone. Who
are we around others? How do we respond to a remark, a
comment, or a conversation we don't like? That's our work.

-Emily Maroutian

#59 – Advice

Seeing a partner as someone you need to conquer or "win" over leaves you in a lonely position. Instead of having a mate you can build your life with, you are left with a conquest you have to fight or work to keep around. It's an exhausting process that will leave you drained and inauthentic. Instead, choose a partner in life who will choose you too, not someone you had to trick or force into a relationship with lies, mind games, or by pretending to be someone else. Those people won't be around for long anyway.

Do you want someone who wants you too or someone who got tricked into being with you? And if you do feel the need to use tricks, what is that saying about how you really think of yourself? If you have to behave in an inauthentic manner to be in a relationship with someone, you are saying that you are not worthy of real love.

-Emily Maroutian

#60 – Lesson

Life is as bland or as magical as we think it is. A flower can be a simple aspect of nature that we walk by every day and don't even notice, or it can be so intricately beautiful that it awakens revelations within us. Our relationship with life depends on how we look at the simple things, which aren't simple at all.

-Emily Maroutian

#61 – Quote

Gratitude and fear are mutually exclusive. They cannot exist in the same space in your life. Where one is fed, the other diminishes.

-Emily Maroutian

#62 – Advice

Not everyone seeks peace or joy in their relationships. Some people have only known negativity as a normal occurrence, argument as communication, criticism and aggression as love, or combativeness as a natural way of being. They don't believe those other things are even possible or normal. They've only experienced one type of behavior as love. You have to decide if that's what you consider love as well. If not, you must be brave enough to move on and find someone who speaks the same love language as you.

-Emily Maroutian

#63 – Lesson

There are some things you have to let happen and some things you have to make happen. The wisdom is in knowing which is which because you can spend years working on the wrong one in the wrong way and not have anything happen.

-Emily Maroutian

#64 – Quote

The divine rests in you too. You can call it your soul or spirit, but it's there and it's in everyone else as well. Whatever it is you've been through here, whatever path you've trekked, whatever reasons you may have for your behavior, it doesn't measure up to the expansive divinity that rests in you. It doesn't matter how many battles you wage; the only thing ever worth winning already exists in you. There is an ounce of God in you, and it is a million times more powerful than all your humanness.

-Emily Maroutian

#65 – Advice

People might not like you when you're in your transitional stage. You might be up, then down, angry one minute, happy the next. You might be confused about the direction of your life and have jumbled thoughts but then get really clear about what you should be doing. You might want to be social but then crave solitude and not want to see anyone for a while. People might not get you, and that's okay. When you become what you're in the process of becoming, you will see that it was all worth it. All the right people will still be around. They will see what you have become, and they will love you still.

-Emily Maroutian

#66 – Lesson

The years are going to pass whether you go back to school or quit your job to live your passion. Whether you take a chance on something new or play it safe in a job you hate. Whether you break up with someone you no longer love or stay together out of habit and comfort. Your life is happening right here, right now. It is every day, every decision, and every moment. And they all add up to the years that are passing now.

-Emily Maroutian

#67 – Quote

There is no shortage of energy in the universe. Everything you feel, which is a request, can flow to you if you are in a state of allowing for that request. It's all about matching energies. There is no such thing as denial, only focused energy being allowed or resisted by you.

-Emily Maroutian

#68 – Advice

A million different people will expect a million different things from you, and you can't be everything to everyone. You have to pick and choose based on which expectation lines up with your own expectation of yourself. Stay true to your own dream of you.

-Emily Maroutian

#69 – Lesson

You can't heal yourself by hurting others. Spreading pain doesn't heal anyone—it only creates more wounded people.

-Emily Maroutian

#70 – Quote

Some people come into our lives as booster engines. They help us get off the ground, they propel us forward, and then they fall away. Sometimes, there's a lot of heat and fire. Sometimes, it's a struggle. We think that the relationship was a failure or it didn't "work" because the person couldn't stay. When in reality, it did exactly what it was meant to do: boost us up and fall away. Now, you are in orbit.

-Emily Maroutian

#71 – Advice

Don't change who you are as an emotional response to someone else. If an angry person makes you angry, then you become like him. Respond to him as you are, not as he is.

-Emily Maroutian

#72 – Lesson

No one can ever understand the full you. They will only see, hear, and comprehend whichever piece that matches with what they're seeking, expecting, or able to understand from the context of their own lives. If they only focus on the negatives, that is a reflection of their own consciousness and is not about you. You are multidimensional, expansive, and layered. Most importantly, you are always growing. Other people's judgments don't encompass you; they don't define you. It reveals more about them than it does about you.

-Emily Maroutian

#73 – Quote

Accusing other people of racism, sexism, or any other prejudice doesn't exonerate us from it. Looking down on other people's behavior doesn't make ours more righteous. We have to stop this cultural, social, and spiritual superiority where we point at other people being the perpetrators of the problem while simultaneously excusing ourselves from doing anything about our own involvement. We are also a part of the problem and have to acknowledge it because we have no right to condemn others for what we deny within ourselves.

-Emily Maroutian

#74 – Advice

Find a way to make the process fun, and you will never have to work "hard" ever again. And as you're busy having fun, the results will take care of themselves.

-Emily Maroutian

#75 – Lesson

No experience is ever wrong or a waste. Everything either currently serves you or will serve you in the future. Each experience adds to your being and will culminate into what you will become. It is your becoming.

-Emily Maroutian

#76 – Quote

The revolution is the way you live your life every day, not just a few days of rebellion or senseless violence. It is your growth, your consciousness, and your behavior. It is who you chose to become; it is how you choose to become. It is you or it is nothing. It is a revolution of consciousness, or else it is a useless revolution.

-Emily Maroutian

#77 – Advice

If you narrow your attention on problems, that's all you'll see.
It's all about focus. Notice the possibilities, the opportunities,
even if you don't take them. Just notice them there, and more
will come.

-Emily Maroutian

#78 – Lesson

People who advise you to be realistic are only talking about their real. Your real is different. What you want to do is probably far more realistic in your world than in theirs. You can't judge your life from other people's limitations. You can't live your life the way they live theirs. We all have different roads and opportunities and possibilities. If the idea came to you on your road, then it has a possibility of becoming real for you. All real things were once just thoughts that someone chose to act upon. If you view your road from someone else's obstructed view of your road, you won't see much possibility in anything.

-Emily Maroutian

#79 – Quote

Regret is disempowering because it focuses the present onto something from the past that can't be changed. It strips us of our power in the moment and fills us with negativity, ruining what we currently have. This does nothing to change what has happened; it only changes what is happening.

-Emily Maroutian

#80 – Advice

If you say you want the truth, you have to be willing to hear what the other person is saying regardless of whether it agrees with your own truth. It's the same with asking people to be open with you. It might not look like what you're expecting but if you asked, you must be willing to accept it as it is.

Accepting it doesn't necessarily mean you are now stuck with it. You are welcome to choose other, more suitable options for yourself, but don't insult or reject the person for their truth or for not matching your idea of it.

-Emily Maroutian

#81 – Lesson

If we have to attack someone else just to make ourselves feel
safe, we'll only create more danger. If we have to disrespect
others just to make ourselves look better, we'll only look
worse. If we have to persecute other people for their beliefs
just to make ours more righteous, we'll only make it more
wicked. Other people have nothing to do with how we feel
about ourselves, our lives, or our beliefs. All doubts,
insecurities, and prejudices come from within us and have
little to do with what other people are doing. We have to
work from within. We have to start with ourselves.

-Emily Maroutian

#82 – Quote

Unconditional love is about the removal of conditions on your emotions. It's about not allowing the behavior of other people to dictate how you feel. Love is something that happens within you, just like anger or sadness. So the idea that other people "cause" emotions is the hindrance to unconditional love.

-Emily Maroutian

#83 – Advice

When you tune into a specific channel on the radio or on TV,
you expect a certain type of programming or music from that
channel. It's the same with our lives. If you keep bumping
into people who cause drama, betray you, or lie, then you have
to change something within your schedule of programming.
You are the channel that pulls in the viewers. You have to
change your stories to change your listeners. It's your
broadcast that is attracting those people to tune into you. It
matches what they want, like, or are attracted to. Change the
quality of your programming and watch how your listeners
and viewers change as well.

-Emily Maroutian

#84 – Lesson

At fifteen, you don't want the same things you wanted when you were ten. At twenty-five, you don't want the same things you wanted when you were fifteen. And five or ten years from now, you're not going to want the same things you want now. Life causes people to expand and grow, and we don't always want what we desired before. It's okay to walk away from jobs, people, or relationships you've outgrown.

People use the word loyalty like it's a jail sentence, as if you're always going to be happy with a decision you made at twenty or even thirty. You're a work in progress, and you're allowed to grow. Your desires are allowed to change. Your decisions are not final. Nothing in life is final—not even death. All of life is evolution and change. And in a few years, you will not be the same person who said yes, or no, or I do. That's the only guarantee in life: it will change

-Emily Maroutian

#85 – Quote

The threat isn't out there in some other country; it's the prejudice in our own minds. It's what we do in our own backyards. It's how we talk to ourselves. It's how we treat our own family members and neighbors. It's how we behave every day.

-Emily Maroutian

#86 – Advice

What you accept in the behavior of others will always show you how you really feel about yourself. Do you find yourself constantly making excuses for other people's bad behavior?

Do you accept abuse as a form of love? These are all indicators of a lack of self-love. Love yourself enough to not allow anyone to hurt you repeatedly. Love yourself enough to leave situations and people who are not worthy of you. Love yourself enough to choose the type of people who love you too.

-Emily Maroutian

#87 – Lesson

When I was a child and took Karate lessons, one of the first things we learned was how to fall properly. It was a mandatory exercise because falling was expected. We were going to get hit, and some of those hits would naturally result in a fall. The key was to fall in such a way as to minimize the damage to ourselves. We learned that falling did not automatically mean pain. We didn't have to stay down there, to feel bad, or to feel defeated. We just needed to accept it as a normal part of engaging with someone else. We expected it. So we learned how to fall gracefully. We learned how to fall lightly. And I never forgot that life lesson. If you learn how to fall properly, you won't ever spend a minute fearing the possible pain of it. You won't live your life avoiding the people and areas in your life that might cause it. Instead, you embrace what's in front of you, you ride the adventure, and when it's time to fall, you fall gracefully. Then you get back up.

-Emily Maroutian

#88 – Quote

As we grow, we grow into new ways of being, which brings about new challenges. We reach new levels of understanding that present new problems. As we grow out of one issue, we are presented with another that better suits our new perspective. Nothing about this process means that something has gone wrong. It's a natural progression; we're merely evolving.

-Emily Maroutian

#89 – Advice

We all want someone to take an interest in us, to ask about what we think and feel. Nothing makes us feel more valued than when someone is fascinated enough to inquire about who we are. It's one of the best gifts we can give each other. When given the opportunity, ask questions, and then to listen to the answers. Each life is a story, a movie, or a book; there's something fascinating and unique about it. Revel in it.

-Emily Maroutian

#90 – Lesson

People can't love us enough to fix our low self-esteem. They can't think highly enough of us to give us a sense of worthiness or compliment us enough to fill those holes. They'll only exhaust themselves trying because that's not their job. Nothing will ever feel enough because the only thing we're ever really missing is our own love. Self-love is a self-job, and anyone else who tries to love enough to make up for our own lack will only place a Band-Aid on an infected wound.

-Emily Maroutian

#91 – Quote

If you feel angry about an issue, then it's not healed within you. Anger is an indicator of an open wound. But anger will not heal it because it's not medicine. It's there as a gauge to show you what needs attention and healing. It's not the cure; it's the diagnosis.

-Emily Maroutian

#92 – Advice

Joy and suffering are simply a matter of where you direct your
attention. Don't choose to focus on the aspects that frustrate
you and seem impossible to accomplish; you might think
you're being rational or logical, but you're merely talking
yourself out of something you really want. The inability to see
a solution in the moment does not mean it doesn't exist.
Focus on what works and more will work.

-Emily Maroutian

#93 – Lesson

When we like a certain TV show, a type of music, a different
lifestyle, or even the same sex, we have to remember that it's
just as valid and important as other people's likes and desires.
We shouldn't feel embarrassed about our preferences. Maybe
we need it; maybe it saves us, comforts us, or heals us. Maybe
it fills a hole we don't have other ways of filling quite yet.
Maybe it offers us a light on our darkest days. Maybe it's
exactly what we're meant to like in the moment we like it.
Others may not understand it, but it's not their place to
understand or validate it. It's not about them. It's about
what's happening within us, and that's just as important as
what's happening within them. It merely shows up differently.

-Emily Maroutian

#94 – Quote

The worst hate is hate disguised as goodness. It gets inside good people who think they're doing the right thing by discriminating. It is also often disguised as protection, and so we think we're doing something valuable. However, we become willing to sacrifice other people's humanity for our own false sense of safety, leaving no one good or safe. We must do what is right above doing what is safe.

-Emily Maroutian

#95 – Advice

Say no as often as it feels right to say it. There is immense power in the word that is greatly underutilized by people who end up becoming sick as a result. Life will teach you to say it if you can't find the courage. And if life won't, your body will.

-Emily Maroutian

#96 – Lesson

Life has a way of redirecting you back onto your path when you become distracted by the idea of things that are not you.

If you stray too far toward the edges, it will find a way to bump you back. Sometimes, it does it through an accident, or a breakup, or a loss of some sort. Usually, it comes in the form of a "no." Either way, you eventually gain the clarity you were lacking and continue to move in *your* direction as opposed to trying to mimic or copy someone else's. There is no such thing as rejection, only redirection.

-Emily Maroutian

#97 – Quote

Cynicism serves no one except the cynic. It's an easy out. It's a safe place, but nothing worthwhile ever comes from there. First, you must dare to believe.

-Emily Maroutian

#98 – Advice

Approach every issue with a calm mind. If you're angry or
upset about a problem, don't approach it yet. Find an
appropriate way to release those emotions before you sit with
it. Regardless of how angry you get with a problem or a
person, it will never fix the issue or the relationship. Anger is
not a remedy; it is a perpetuator of the problem. Release it
first and then approach the problem.

-Emily Maroutian

#99 – Lesson

Your surroundings reflect your energy. Changing them isn't always the answer. You can step into a new place with all of your old problems, issues, traumas, and dramas. And what will end up happening is you will attract similar people who keep it cycling in your life. If you change the surroundings before you're energetically different, you'll just attract the same situations with different faces.

-Emily Maroutian

#100 – Quote

If you feel angry with someone else for saying something you don't like, it's showing you that you place far too much value on other people's opinions and judgments and not enough on your own. It's an opportunity to begin building value for your own time, energy, and opinions and let go of others control over you.

-Emily Maroutian

#101 – Advice

Use negative emotion as a guide and nothing more. Use it as an opportunity for clarity. It will show you point blank where you are on a topic. If you feel jealous of another's relationship, it's showing you that you really believe you can't have that for yourself. That's an opportunity to clear up the emotional gunk in that area and work on your self-esteem and worthiness. If you feel angry with any subject, it shows you have more work to do to heal it. Let it guide you to where you need the work. And when you get there, don't look around and get angry with yourself for it—just clean it up.

-Emily Maroutian

#102 – Lesson

We often confuse suffering and contrast. Contrast is a law
and fact in the universe; up will have down, in will have out,
black will have white, pleasure will have pain. It doesn't mean
we have to suffer for one and rejoice in the other. Thinking
you are only supposed to experience one your whole life and
should avoid the other is what creates suffering. When you
accept both as necessities of life, you will find more peace
within yourself.

-Emily Maroutian

#103 – Quote

On a daily basis, we come across children and teens with unresolved pain. They fight us to find some kind of resolution within them. They pull us into their drama so they don't feel so alone in it. They push us and throw emotional tantrums because they don't understand what's unresolved or unhealed. But most importantly, they walk around in adult bodies so no one else really listens or understands.

-Emily Maroutian

#104 – Advice

There's no value in beating yourself up for mistakes made in the past. Just the mere fact that you now recognize them as mistakes shows how much you've grown and expanded from whom you used to be. Celebrate that; don't make yourself wrong for it. That's normal. It's the nature of growth.

-Emily Maroutian

#105 – Lesson

All wounds naturally want to heal. What you leave unresolved will fight for your attention. The more you ignore it, the harder it'll fight. It will mirror the problem and pain through spouses, bosses, children, parents, or friends. It will pull at you and push at you until you can look at it, heal it, and move on. No other action will satisfy it because a wound's only desire is to be healed. When we give it the proper attention and care, it will never bother us again.

-Emily Maroutian

#106 – Quote

The inherent value of any religion or philosophy appears in the behavior of its followers. Your life and behavior represent what you believe. No one outside of the religion can promote or destroy it. That power belongs only to its followers.

-Emily Maroutian

#107 – Advice

Limited thinking keeps you in limited space. Doors and paths don't open until you're open. If you want more opportunities, you have to be open enough to see them all around you.

-Emily Maroutian

#108 – Lesson

If you leave yourself behind, others will leave you behind too.
If you lie to yourself, others will lie to you too. If you don't
pay attention to your own needs, others won't either. How
you treat yourself sets the example for others.

-Emily Maroutian

#109 – Quote

Everything that exists now was once just a thought in someone's mind. Thoughts become ideas, which become passions, which become goals, which become reality. A thought or an idea is not enough to make a dream come true, but it's crucial to the birth of the dream. It is the conception point of all advancement.

-Emily Maroutian

#110 – Advice

You can always gauge what is going to come back from your choices based on how you feel as you're choosing. Are you filled with fear, possible regret, anxiety, or dread? Do you feel right, peaceful, content, or hopeful? Your feelings infuse your energy into the decision you're making, and you receive back the equivalent of the energy you sent out. Never rush a decision. Take some time to find ease first. Wait until you feel better, and then choose.

-Emily Maroutian

Great art is created in a moment of pure unrestricted self-expression. It shifts you. It makes you feel. It makes you think. It might even upset you. It is inspiring, free-flowing, and unrestrained. It is beautiful even in its ugliness.

Real art pulls out emotions. Whether it's bad, sick, uncomfortable, happy, joyful, or depressed. It makes you feel because it is reflecting what's inside. Art does not cause negativity; it brings suppressed negativity to the surface so that it can be healed.

-Emily Maroutian

#112 – Advice

Worrying is a lack of self-trust. It's saying you don't believe you are strong or smart enough to handle what happens in your life. That's not true because you've survived everything in your life so far and there is no indication that you won't do that again and again. Trust yourself.

-Emily Maroutian

#113 – Lesson

Distrust is a form of insecurity. People seem to think that trust has something to do with the other person's behavior when really trust is about the self. Do you trust yourself to survive after a break-up? Do you trust yourself to be able to pick yourself back up and move on? Do you trust your strength? Do you trust your intelligence? Do you trust yourself to be okay? If the answer to all of these questions is yes, then you never need to distrust anyone. Distrust is the fear of an unwanted outcome. But if you trust yourself to be able to handle anything that comes your way, the fear of any unwanted outcome can't control you ever again.

-Emily Maroutian

#114 – Quote

To forgive is to clear space for new people and experiences to enter your life. If you continue to carry the past into your present, you will recycle those painful experiences into your next one. Forgiveness isn't about the murky past—it's about a clear future.

-Emily Maroutian

#115 – Advice

The best support you can give to anyone you love is your wellness. When you are well, joyful, fun, and happy, you are the greatest gift to everyone around you. That's when you inspire wellness, joy, and fun within them. When you take care of yourself, you are in a much better position to take care of others.

Your tiredness, sickness, and inability to look after yourself does not support or help anyone. Your loved ones don't want to be the cause of your unhappiness or exhaustion. They want to be the cause of your joy and wellness. That's the same reason you take care of them—you want them to be joyful and well. Words don't teach as well as example. Support others through your thriving. Lift others by lifting yourself.

-Emily Maroutian

#116 – Lesson

If you don't take time for yourself now, you'll spend most of
your time later working on healing a tired and sick body along
with an exhausted mind. Self-care is not just needed and wise;
it's also time efficient. There is no such thing as wasting time
doing something relaxing. If you don't do it every once in a
while, you'll be forced to do it when your body runs out of
fuel and becomes ill.

-Emily Maroutian

#117 – Quote

You can't wait for others to give you the love and acceptance you want. The validation you're seeking is from yourself. It's the only opinion that matters in your world.

-Emily Maroutian

#118 – Advice

Restriction does not create loyalty; freedom does. People are more likely to stay with someone who gives them freedom and trust than with someone who is restrictive, controlling, and limiting. No one wants to commit or dedicate themselves to their jailers; it only creates resentment and makes them want to break free.

Freedom, not restriction, creates trust. Anyone can trust a caged person not to go anywhere, but can you trust a free person to come back? Also, if all of your partners need to be caged to be loyal to you, then what does that say about how you feel about yourself?

Let go, trust, and know that you'll be okay regardless of who does what. When you trust yourself, you'll be able to trust others as well. When you free yourself, you'll only want those who are free as well.

-Emily Maroutian

#119 – Lesson

So often, we place too much emphasis on things "lasting," as if the value of the thing is attached to the length of time it is in our lives. Everything serves its purpose and then falls away. Whether it's a job or a relationship, no experience in life is wasteful. It may take us years to learn its true value, but everything adds to our evolution as it's happening. One thing leads to another and another. We don't go straight from A to Z; there's a whole journey in between. Each relationship prepares us for the next. One thing opens the way to another.

-Emily Maroutian

#120 – Quote

We can destroy our relationships simply by having the fear of destroying our relationships. We can fail at our businesses simply by having the fear of failing at our businesses. Fear is a powerful emotion that focuses energy into the direction of the thing we don't want. We often create it by fearing it.

-Emily Maroutian

#121 – Advice

Teach children to speak up, to trust their own intuition, to make their own choices. Teach them that mistakes don't mean that they are bad or wrong or stupid. Teach them to trust themselves, to care for themselves, to say no, to never betray themselves just to please others.

Teaching love and confidence is not teaching "better than" thinking. You're not teaching them that they are above others; you're teaching them that they matter too. That's the difference between raising a child who has self-love vs. self-hate, confidence vs. arrogance, generosity vs. greed, a happy, fulfilling life vs. a miserable one.

-Emily Maroutian

#122 – Lesson

You can't force, push, insult, or bomb people into peace and love. In the same way, you can't abuse yourself into alignment. Negative means produce negative results. You have to ease yourself into acceptance. You have to accept yourself into love. You have to love yourself into peace. You have to peace yourself into joy. And once you've successfully transformed your own aggressive and judgmental mind, you will then know how to change the world.

-Emily Maroutian

#123 – Quote

In life, you have to be confident but not forceful, easy-going but purposeful, focused but open-minded, and centered in your own self but compassionate toward others. There is a middle ground to being that when achieved will make your life easier and richer than it has ever been.

-Emily Maroutian

#124 – Advice

They say other people's negativity is like poison, and what I know about poison is that it can't hurt you unless you take it in. Don't swallow other people's words thinking they're better nourishment than your own. Don't breath in other people's judgments thinking it's cleaner or fresher than your own. Don't let any of it enter your skin by leaving your wounds open and unhealed. Most importantly, don't stay in any place or with anyone that offers you poison.

-Emily Maroutian

#125 – Lesson

If we don't heal our childhood wounds, we'll carry them into our adult relationships and try to get from our partners now what we didn't get then.

-Emily Maroutian

#126 – Quote

Everything is always in a permanent state of transformation and change. This means that everything is temporary in an eternal way. So, even though nothing lasts, everything lasts.

-Emily Maroutian

#127 – Advice

We often think that by saying no, we're denying something to someone else, but we don't seem to mind that we're denying our own integrity, voice, power, and choice by saying yes to something we don't want.

We are so afraid to use the word no because we believe we'll wound others with it. However, not using it has the power to move us into something we don't want and make us give up our time and energy because we can't say it to others. In some ways, we wound ourselves.

Use it. Say no as often as you feel inclined to. It is your right to choose what you do with your time and energy. Whoever doesn't understand that and wants to force you for their own benefit doesn't respect your power of choice and shouldn't be given the opportunity to disrespect it again.

-Emily Maroutian

#128 – Lesson

You can't make people regret leaving you. It doesn't matter how well you live or what you do, people move on and they find ways to justify their past actions. The best thing you can do for yourself is move on too.

-Emily Maroutian

#129 – Quote

I want to love who you really are, not the person you think I
would love. You have no idea so don't guess, don't assume,
don't change yourself. You might be exactly what I'm looking
for and I don't want to miss the opportunity to know you
because you changed yourself to impress me.

-Emily Maroutian

#130 – Advice

Confidence in yourself and your decisions doesn't require validation or agreement from others. Don't be afraid to choose; you can't get it wrong because there is always another choice and another and another.

-Emily Maroutian

#131 – Lesson

People think that enlightenment is about being positive and optimistic all the time, as if we are supposed to give up all other emotions because they are beneath us now. Enlightenment is a type of conscious waking up. It is about the awareness we have around the things we feel; it is not a relinquishing of emotions.

Are you aware of why you became upset? Can you see how you created that situation? Do you understand the core of your sadness? Yes, once you become aware you will feel and behave differently, that's a given, but it won't automatically heal all of your wounds and stop negative emotion. That's why you need the awareness—because now the work begins. Enlightenment is just the beginning; it is not a final destination.

-Emily Maroutian

#132 – Quote

We think that fame or wealth are going to be the cures for our unhappiness, loneliness, or unworthiness, when really they are the amplifiers of anything we have unresolved or unhealed within us. They will pull our issues into the forefront for all to see until we are willing to deal with it and heal it. Fame and money don't heal; they reveal.

-Emily Maroutian

#133 – Advice

Needing to be right all the time is a symptom of low self-esteem. When we feel our own worth is being attacked as a result of an opposing view, we are really saying that who we are must be validated by others for it to be true. Anyone who is confident in who they are doesn't base their worthiness on other people's agreement.

Let go of the disease of "rightness" and accept that everyone has their own unique perspective. Just because it doesn't agree with your own doesn't make it more or less wrong.

-Emily Maroutian

#134 – Lesson

Changing laws doesn't change sexism, racism, or homophobia.
It just makes it illegal to act on it. It doesn't change the
hearts and minds of people. That has to happen on an
individual level through heart-to-heart dialogue.

-Emily Maroutian

#135 – Quote

If you're ever going to be two with someone, you have to be a full one by yourself.

-Emily Maroutian

#136 – Advice

Beliefs are more powerful than dreams or desires. If they happen to contradict each other, beliefs will win each time. In working toward your dreams, also work on the beliefs that hinder them or else you'll be working against yourself.

-Emily Maroutian

#137 – Lesson

Are you asking that question because you want to know an
answer, or are you asking that question because you want an
opportunity to defend what you already believe? Are you
trying to goad someone into an argument, or are you
genuinely open and curious about another perspective? If you
can honestly answer those questions, then you'll know why
you're always angry with other people's beliefs. Why you
always feel attacked and defensive. Everyone wants to change
other people's minds, but no one wants their mind changed.
It simply doesn't work that way. We don't learn that way. We
stay the same that way.

-Emily Maroutian

#138 – Quote

People can inspire us to find our own voice, happiness, freedom, love, or peace, but they can't give it to us. It is offered only as a thought, an idea, or inspiration, and it is up to us to take it and follow through. In the same way, others can't influence us negatively unless we take it and follow through on it.

-Emily Maroutian

#139 – Advice

People might not understand your depression because you have more food, shelter, and fresh water compared to less fortunate people in the world. They'll say, "Look at all you have; you have nothing to be depressed about." But you are more than just your physical needs and that alone is not enough to guarantee happiness. You may not be physically hungry, but your soul might be starving.

Give yourself the permission to feel whatever it is that you feel as you work it all out. This is your journey. No one else can justify or invalidate your emotions about it.

-Emily Maroutian

#140 – Quote

You can't really "wait" for someone because you can't place
your growth on hold. You can slow it down, but it never
stops. By the time they come around, you will most likely be a
different person. And maybe that person just doesn't want
any of those things anymore.

-Emily Maroutian

#141 – Advice

As the father of a girl, scaring and intimidating boys who date her won't keep her safe because she is the one who picks the type of boys she dates. And scaring one bad boy away will only make room for another. So trying to create rules for the boys' behaviors is only a temporary means of protection because if she's attracted to boys who treat her horribly, then no amount of rules can change anything. However, if you raise her with confidence, self-love, and show her through your own example how a man is supposed to treat her, then she will shut down anyone who tries otherwise. She will choose better mates, ones who remind her of her own worth and how great her father treated her. You don't need rules or to scare boys into behaving; simply raise confident daughters. They'll take care of themselves. Empower your daughters instead of scaring their boyfriends.

-Emily Maroutian

#142 – Lesson

The most effective way to eliminate negativity from our lives is not to eliminate the people we think cause it but to eliminate the negativity that is already within ourselves. People can't pull out or trigger anything that isn't already there. They can only trigger old wounds we haven't yet healed. It's an opportunity to heal—not to blame.

-Emily Maroutian

#143 – Quote

Violence is not a proper argument. It has only one objective:
make it impossible for the other side to express its point of
view. It shuts down communication and closes off any
possibility of debate. Without genuine dialogue, no real
progress can be made on either side.

-Emily Maroutian

#144 – Advice

Don't say yes to something even though you would rather say no because that is an act of self-betrayal. If you do that long enough, then you create the energy of betrayal within you and keep it dominant in your experience. Soon enough, others will betray you as well; they'll say "yes, I will be truthful," but they'll really mean "No, I won't." They'll say, "I do" when they really mean they don't. Our energetic habits create the experiences we get back, and a lot of that begins with how we treat ourselves.

-Emily Maroutian

#145 – Quote

Bullies have a lot of pain that they don't know any other way
of releasing. They simply weren't taught healthy self-
expression or conflict resolution. Punishment keeps them
stuck in the cycle of anger and powerlessness, which makes
them continue to lash out at others. They don't need to be
punished; they need to be healed. There is no excuse for the
behavior; however, there is a reason for it and that's where we
have to look for a real solution.

-Emily Maroutian

#146 – Advice

Ask yourself if your choices are based on fear or desire. Are you choosing what you want, or are you choosing to avoid what you fear? Did you choose one thing because you didn't want the other, or did you choose it because that's the one you wanted? The difference between those two will determine your overall happiness with the outcome.

-Emily Maroutian

#147 – Lesson

There's a lot of destruction that happens with enlightenment because there is a peeling-away process, a removal of unnecessary characteristics and habits that we picked up for defense or survival. We often find that we don't want to play those games anymore. We don't want to pretend or lie. Not to others and not to ourselves.

-Emily Maroutian

#148 – Quote

Thoughts are electrical, and emotions are magnetic. The thoughts we think charge up our emotions, which then pulls in matching energy in the form of an experience.

-Emily Maroutian

#149 – Advice

Your inability to process or accept someone else is an issue within yourself and has nothing to do with them. They are not inconceivable or unacceptable; you are just reacting to an issue within yourself. It's your inner battle; they're just a symbol.

Don't use them as the target for your own misunderstandings or ignorance. Other people are not responsible for what is happening within you. They are not responsible for what you don't understand, like, or accept. Your emotions belong to you. Your response is your response-ability.

-Emily Maroutian

#150 – Lesson

If you don't value your own opinions, you will always seek validation from others. You will look to them to confirm your beliefs. You will look to them to compliment you and lift your emotions higher. You will look to them to guide your life and approve of your goals.

Other people don't need to give you permission to feel good about yourself. Who you are is just as enough as they are. If their opinions are valuable, so are yours. If they matter, so do you. If their beliefs are powerful, so are yours. The only imbalance that happens among people is in their own minds.

-Emily Maroutian

#151 – Quote

Everything we want in life is because we want the emotion behind the goal. We want to feel accomplished, happy, powerful, and good. So we want the car, the house, the spouse, and the money because they will bring us those emotions. All goals are really emotions disguised as things.

-Emily Maroutian

#152 – Advice

When you inspire yourself, you inspire others as well. Your
enthusiasm, passion, and energy become contagious to the
people around you. People won't be able to help it; when they
see you thriving, it'll trigger their desire to thrive as well.
Follow your compass of joy, and you'll do more for people
than if you stayed behind and attempted to please them.

-Emily Maroutian

#153 – Lesson

It takes maturity to stop pretending, to stop looking for confirmation, to stop bending ourselves into other people's visions of us. We never fully grow up until we grow into ourselves. We are never fully ourselves until we give up being what's convenient for others.

-Emily Maroutian

#154 – Quote

There may be an imbalance of money among people, but there is never an imbalance of worth or importance. Every human being can create and add great value in the lives of others. We all have access to the people around us, and we can always start there. We don't have to wait until we have more of this or less of that. We can do it here, and we can do it now.

-Emily Maroutian

#155 – Advice

There's a difference between questions that seek connection
and questions that seek battles. Some questions are designed
to push people into arguments because we feel vulnerable and
therefore defensive. We think the only way we're going to
retain any kind of control in our lives is through proving
others wrong. We feel we have to be right in this particular
argument and we just can't seem to let it go. We enter into a
battle for power and control because we feel neither in the
moment.

Stay aware in your communication with people and gauge
where you stand emotionally within each topic. Are you
looking for connection or power? Either one is an indication
of what you're currently lacking because if you had it, you
wouldn't seek it out.

-Emily Maroutian

#156 – Lesson

Your very first relationship is not with your parents; it's with yourself. You are your first love affair, your first relationship, and the first opinion that ever mattered. If you take in other people's opinions about yourself and allow them to change how you feel, you'll change the most important relationship in your life. If it becomes a bad one, an abusive one, a negative one, it will set the standard for everyone else. All relationships that follow will mirror that first relationship.

-Emily Maroutian

#157 – Quote

Illness can be a form of hiding. It gives us a valid excuse to get out of doing things that go against who we are and what we want to do with our lives. The more we stifle our own creativity and unique voice, the sicker we become. If there is no personal freedom, there is no personal wellness.

-Emily Maroutian

#158 – Lesson

If others challenge our truth with facts or evidence against it, we won't be able to hear it clearly because we only accept the truth that matches and confirms our own. We'll find intellectual ways around it, argue against them, call them names, cut them out of our lives, even become violent, but we won't accept what we don't want to accept or are not ready to accept.

This is why we can't ever argue people into our beliefs or perspectives. Those who are ready to hear us won't require an argument, and those who can't hear us won't hear us any better when we start shouting. At some point, everyone learns the emotional difference between feeling peaceful and needing to be right.

-Emily Maroutian

#159 – Quote

If a war in raging in your mind, how can you create peace in your life? It all begins in the mind and takes shape through our actions and behaviors. A mind full of rage doesn't create a relationship full of peace.

-Emily Maroutian

#160 – Lesson

Benjamin Franklin observed that when he walked into a room and a group of men laughed at him or made a snarky remark, all he would have to do is approach those men and engage in a friendly conversation about something. Sometimes, it was the weather; sometimes, it was a personal compliment. It was his understanding that people who hated him really only wanted to be a part of his greatness but felt like outsiders. They felt left out. This jealousy turned them into haters. However, once they were given the opportunity to feel connected, included, and acknowledged, they became fans and even friends. Benjamin Franklin became known as a master at killing hate with kindness.

-Emily Maroutian

#161 – Quote

Going through shit enhances your growth in the same way manure enhances the growth of plants. Lessons aren't always pretty and fun to go through. In most cases, they're the opposite. It's dark, lonely, and a struggle to push through, but once you see the light past the dirt, you bloom like you've never bloomed before.

-Emily Maroutian

#162 – Advice

Don't ask your child to devolve into an image of something you recognize and are comfortable with. That goes against their evolution, growth, and reason for being. They're not here to make you comfortable or to become the extensions of your mentality. They're born in a new time, in a new world, and they are meant for different things. They're not here to support your old ways; they're here to help you grow into something new.

-Emily Maroutian

#163 – Lesson

We are all uplifters and motivators deep down inside. We get our true sense of personal power from offering others hope and inspiration. We want to know that others benefited from their experience with us. We want to know that we made a positive impact on them. We want to know that our lives matter within the big picture.

But when we can't find a positive way to express that need, we turn to the opposite means. We belittle and put others down. We criticize them and make them feel as small as we do. We try to feel that same uplifting power through negative ways, which doesn't work.

Negative power is not the same as positive power. It doesn't sooth the need for upliftment and positive impact, which can't stay silent and unfulfilled for too long. It must be expressed eventually and so it pushes us to act in any way we can. The need for that personal power is so commanding that we will settle for having a negative impact instead of no impact at all.

-Emily Maroutian

#164 – Quote

Every moment prepares us for the next one and the next one.
We are never handed anything we aren't already familiar with
on some level. If we feel as if something is beyond our power,
it just means we haven't been paying attention to our own
growth.

-Emily Maroutian

#165 – Lesson

We spend too much time and energy trying to get other people to understand what we mean or how we feel, almost as if it's not important unless we have some kind of agreement from others. You don't require anyone else's understanding to think, feel, do, or be. That is a people-pleasing disease we learned in childhood. "Explain yourself. What do you mean? What were you thinking? Why did you do that?"

We hand over the power of our choices by explaining ourselves so that others can understand us and feel better about our actions. You don't need other people to feel better about your actions. How do you feel? That's the only question of value.

-Emily Maroutian

Feminism isn't about women having power over men; it's about women having power over themselves. Over their own bodies, wellbeing, education, careers, and motherhood. It's about the opportunity of choice, whether she chooses to stay at home, go to school, not get married, serve her husband, or become the president of a company. It's about having the power to choose her path, whatever it may be. It's not about dominating men; it's about her having dominion over herself.

-Emily Maroutian

#167 – Advice

All forms of art are subjective. Whether it's music, movies, books, or paintings, the value and importance of it will depend on the observer. Everything that is created can be loved and hated at the same time by different people. There is someone out there who will feel it on the deepest levels and another who won't see any beauty in it.

If you come across a piece of creation and you don't like it, then it's not for you. It's as simple as that. Just move on. There is no point in taking time and energy to insult it, criticize it, or tear it down. Instead, find something that does fit. Find something you like that feels more you. There is no bad art; there is only art that matches our feelings or doesn't.

-Emily Maroutian

#168 – Lesson

One of the most important aspects of healing is self-forgiveness. If we can forgive ourselves for our role in what occurred, we can let go of our internal need to blame and victimize ourselves. We can stop making ourselves sick as a form of punishment.

Most of the time we think we're mad at others, but we're really mad at ourselves. Whether it's because we trusted people who betrayed us, believed in lies, allowed behavior we didn't like, or didn't see what we think we should have seen, most anger is directed at the self. Anytime there's still pain about a past situation, it requires some level of self-forgiveness.

-Emily Maroutian

#169 – Quote

It's not the judgment of others that bothers us the most but
our own judgment of ourselves. Even when we become
people-pleasers and help everyone around us, what we are
really looking for is our own acknowledgment of worth. We
don't want others to love us; we want to love ourselves. We
want our own approval and acceptance. We're just hoping
that we can convince ourselves to do it by getting agreement
from others.

-Emily Maroutian

Toxic people reflect to us how we feel on the inside. If we feel used, they'll use us. If we feel stupid, small, and unworthy, they will treat us as if we are stupid, small, and unworthy. When we bombard ourselves with critical thoughts and use self-abuse as a means of motivation, others will do the same to us. Toxic people will mirror the toxicity within us. The best way to clean them out of our environment is to clean up how we think and feel about ourselves.

-Emily Maroutian

#171 – Quote

The word God is so loaded with people's established ideas and concepts of what they think it means that they can't hear you talk about it without a ready argument. Those who are open about it remain open about it, and those who are closed about it remain closed about it. There rarely exists a middle ground.

-Emily Maroutian

#172 – Advice

There's freedom in the willingness to look stupid or fail regardless of what other people think of you. You can accomplish more when you are not a prisoner of other people's opinions. If you place too much emphasis on how others see you, you'll never become your full self because you will always be bending and changing to please others. Let go of the need to look a certain way; it is a prison most people never leave.

-Emily Maroutian

#173 – Lesson

Each generation comes in as an evolved version of the one before it. It takes them less time, effort, and energy to learn and create. We judge them harshly for their lack of interest in what matters to us, but it only seems that way because they're born looking at the solutions while we're still busy looking at the problems. We think they don't understand, but it's we who don't understand. They're not rebelling; they're trailblazing. They are evolution; we are habit.

-Emily Maroutian

#174 – Quote

You can't verbally wrestle people into progress. You can't always expect people to be where you are on issues of equality or justice. Their lives and experiences have caused them to draw different conclusions. Sometimes, you have to meet them where they are and guide the conversation to a more inclusive place. Arguing, belittling the other person, or calling them names will never change their hearts or minds because it's in the same combative energy. You have to bring a different energy to get a different result.

-Emily Maroutian

#175 – Advice

Marriage and children are not solutions to insecurity, hardships, depression, or anything else. They are the magnifiers of those things. Your spouse and children will drag out anything that is left unhealed, unloved, and denied within you. Get married, have children only when you are truly ready to face yourself.

-Emily Maroutian

If you look for the easy way because you want to get it over with, more often than not you'll run into the hard way, the delayed way, or the way that asks you to compromise. Looking for the easiest or fastest route usually means there is a lack of interest in doing it in the first place. That resistance toward the task creates delays and problems within it. But if you follow your inner sense of joy and fun regardless of what you're doing, everything will feel easy and will come quickly.

-Emily Maroutian

#177 – Advice

Religion is accepting someone else's experience of God and following their processes, while spirituality is having our own. Every religious book was written by those who had experiences and wrote about it. You don't have to listen, do, or follow anything that doesn't feel right within you. We all have the same access. Have your own experience.

-Emily Maroutian

#178 – Lesson

When you find the great balance that exists within you, you will come alive in ways you had never known was possible. And when you come alive, your life will feel like magic. People will be drawn to you. Things will work out before you even get a chance to think about them. Great opportunities will show up in the funniest "coincidences." People will want to know you, to support you. They will root for you and want you to win. They'll bring you opportunities and avenues for success. They'll respect you and ask you for your advice. They'll see your light and will want to be near it because it feels so good. They'll find you charming and approachable. They'll see something within you that will powerfully pull them in, but they won't be able to explain it. Your presence will bring peace because within you a great peace will exist between opposing forces. And most importantly, you won't care about any of that because you stopped thinking about how others judge you, see you, or feel about you. And that is how you found your balance in the first place.

-Emily Maroutian

#179 – Quote

Fun and obligation move time at different speeds. One speeds
it up, and the other slows it down. Your enjoyment or
suffering in a task will depend on your intention and
perception of it.

-Emily Maroutian

#180 – Advice

You don't have to be right all the time; in fact, you can't. And even when you think you are, it leaves you in an aggressive and combative state, always having to justify and defend your knowledge. It can eat away at your confidence and energy. It doesn't leave you in an open state to learn, grow, and add to your knowledge.

If you think you already know, then you can't let the moment serve you, teach you, and grow you. When you're open to receive, you'll be a better person for having the experience. Learn to let go of the need to be right all the time. It doesn't serve you in any way.

-Emily Maroutian

#181 – Lesson

You don't have to be anyone else's idea of pretty. You don't have to change anything to become more pleasing to someone else's eye. You don't exist to make others comfortable with your beauty. It's not your job to be desired by others. When you feel comfortable in your own skin, your confidence will make you radiate regardless of what you wear or look like. Self-acceptance makes everyone uniquely beautiful.

-Emily Maroutian

#182 – Quote

If the problems of the world could be solved by violence, they already would have been. We would be living in a peaceful utopian society by now with the amount of violence we use as a form of resolution. We need another way. Violence doesn't work; it's a symptom of the problem—not a path to the solution.

-Emily Maroutian

Most of the views we have about our world have been passed down throughout the generations. We keep recreating the old ways without believing in the possibility of change. Our geniuses are really only people who refuse to see the world the way other people do. They see a world that has better technology and so they create better technology. They see a world with solutions and so they create solutions. They believe in a better world and so they better the world. They refuse to accept other people's reality of the world because they see better possibilities. They see what others can't see because they believe *before* they see it, while others only believe after they see it.

-Emily Maroutian

#184 – Lesson

At some point, you have to stop feeling sorry for yourself. You have to stop looking at the world as this unfair place that just takes advantage of you. It very well maybe true that you were a victim of something or another, but so what? Name a person on this earth who hasn't felt that way at least once before. The relevant question is, what are you going to do about it now? That's what distinguishes the leaders, the heroes, the activists, and the warriors. They don't accept anything as a permanent state. They know that everything is changeable for those who have the courage to change it. No one else is going to fight your fight for you. No one else is going create your balance for you. No one else is going to live your life for you. At some point, you have to get up and create your own fairness.

-Emily Maroutian

It's okay to have conflicting thoughts or feelings. It's okay to disagree with others or even with yourself. No one has it all figured out. We're all trying the best we can in each moment. Sometimes, we try something out and receive positive feedback; sometimes, we get negative feedback. None of it means anything about who you are or who others are. There's always another opportunity to get it right and to get it wrong. Life is a succession of successes and failures, rights and wrongs, positivity and negativity. None of it defines you because there's always another chance and another and another.

-Emily Maroutian

#186 – Advice

Let go as often as you can. Let go of expectations, let go of worries, let go of dreams, and let go of people. This doesn't mean stop wanting—it simply means stop holding on to the how's and the when's and the where's. It means stop grasping, stop strangling, stop holding on tightly. It means have faith and let go enough to give it a chance to breathe, flow, and exist. It means let go of everything other than your love.

-Emily Maroutian

#187 – Lesson

There is no separation between the observer and the observed. Once the observer observes something, they are connected in the moment. How you respond through what you observe becomes a part of you. So through your attention to someone else's behavior, you invite that into your experience. You are now upset. You have created upset within you, which will change your day, your emotion, your mood, and how you behave with others. You have now changed because you have observed someone else. He has become a part of your experience through your reaction to him. Whether he is a positive experience or a negative one will depend on you and not him. It depends on your wounds, experiences, pain, and past. It depends on how you view him and not what he does.

-Emily Maroutian

Scientists have calculated that there is a one in four hundred
trillion chance that you were born.
That's 1 in 400,000,000,000,000 with 14 zeros.
And if we factor in all of the past generational events that had
to come together for you to exist, you would see that your life
is a true miracle. Those numbers are miraculous. You are
miraculous.

-Emily Maroutian

#189 – Lesson

Criminals are not the problem with society; they are the effects of the problem. They are created out of a specific environment that breeds them. They are nurtured and fed in the same way cancer has a cause that feeds it and helps it grow and thrive. It is not the cancer we need to fight after the fact, it is the environment we need to correct that creates it. This is the difference between a life-long battle with a problem that keeps reoccurring and implementing an actual solution that stops it from happening in the first place.

-Emily Maroutian

#190 – Quote

People say the best revenge is success, but that implies you're still focused in some way on those people who hurt you. They're still there, influencing you, having power over you. You can't be mentally independent from them and therefore your success is partly an illusion. The best revenge is not caring anymore. It's when they don't even enter your mind, as if they never existed at all. It's independence from the pain and the past. The best revenge is growing out of the person you used to be who was so bothered by them in the first place.

-Emily Maroutian

#191 – Advice

Begin somewhere, anywhere. Just jump in with both feet. Do it even though your heart is pounding. Do it as your body trembles. Do it as you run out of breath. Do it even as you feel the fear or the pain. The greatest changes require leaps of faith.

-Emily Maroutian

#192 – Lesson

When people are being horrible to you, remember that they are the ones being horrible. This is about them. They are offering you an experience of who they are being in the moment. You don't have to accept it, take it, or respond to it. You don't have to do anything that isn't who you are in the moment. Do you want to be horrible too? Do you want to become as they are? Other people's behavior is not your choice, but who you are is.

-Emily Maroutian

#193 – Quote

There's a balance between learning and teaching in life. If you discover it, you will never look at anything as a real problem again. You will approach everything as either an opportunity that is here to teach you something or as an opportunity that is here to learn from you. Anyone at anytime can be standing in front of you as a student or a lesson. If you can distinguish which is which, you can eliminate most of your personal conflicts. Peace exists in understanding this distinction.

-Emily Maroutian

#194 – Advice

Life is as big or as small as your thoughts. You interpret all of the information that comes in, and this creates your experience of it. So if you don't believe something is possible, it won't be. If you have big thoughts, you will have big experiences. If you have small thoughts, you will have small experiences. If you have dramatic thoughts, you will encounter drama. If you have comedic thoughts, even the most dramatic will seem comical to you. Your mind is the filter through which you experience life. You are only as limited as your thinking. All of your present and future experiences will match your mindset every time. Think bigger than you're used to and watch how your life becomes bigger.

-Emily Maroutian

#195 – Lesson

A poor diet in a happy body is far more effective in keeping you well than a healthy diet in a stressed out body. Stress is far more dangerous than any food you could ever eat. It is the cause of more than eighty percent of illnesses. It erodes your immune system, raises your blood sugar and pressure, it changes your hormones, eats your liver, and rewires your brain. It slowly kills you. It is life-threatening to be chronically stressed or fearful, and no amount of healthy foods can fix that. An emotional and mental diet works better than a physical one. A healthy/happy body can process all kinds of food and extract what it needs as it expels what it doesn't. Being careful about what you eat while not being mindful of what you think won't be as effective for your wellness. We need more diets of the mind and fewer diets of the body.

-Emily Maroutian

The world is full of people who hate themselves but don't realize it. Instead, they walk around hurting others. They gossip, bully, abuse, and belittle other people to take away the pain of self-hate. They try to make themselves look and feel important because they feel so very small. They work to plunge the rest of the world into their darkness because they don't want to feel alone in their misery anymore. They influence others through their emotions. We all do.

When you hate yourself, you change everything around you. You change everything you touch or come in contact with. It's the same when you love yourself. You brighten people's lives, you offer more love and magic everywhere you go. Every second of every day you are changing the world. How you feel about yourself determines the type of world you are actively creating.

-Emily Maroutian

#197 – Advice

Read books by people you disagree with. Listen to others who think differently from you. Watch programming you normally wouldn't watch. Expand your mind and views of the world. As right as you think you are about your own beliefs and experiences, others feel the same way about their own. You'll learn more than you ever imagined if you see the world through beliefs rather than right and wrong.

-Emily Maroutian

#198 – Lesson

TV is a powerful medium. It can transport different kinds of people right into your living room, making you feel familiar with their lives. It desensitizes the otherness of the other. If you've only known submissive women, it can show you strong ones. If your environment is exclusively white, it can bring smart, talented, and funny black people right into your house. If you've never spoken to a gay person, it can take you deep into the life of one and show you their happiness and pain. It humanizes people who we might never get a chance to see or meet in real life. TV shows have helped bridge the divide for people who rarely have access to others who are unlike themselves and it shows them just how alike they really are.

-Emily Maroutian

#199 – Quote

Lack of education is not the problem mis-education is. You can be well educated in building bombs and in the philosophies that teach you it's okay to strap them onto yourself and blow other people up. You can be educated in discrimination and hate. You can be educated in false history and blind patriotism. You can be educated to serve false leaders and follow politicians who don't even serve you. It's the mis-education of a mind that creates the divide between people. Most people are educated; they're just educated in things that don't serve the world.

-Emily Maroutian

#200 - Advice

You know what you need better than anyone else. Don't let other people talk you out of your needs or desires. If they're important to you, then they're important. You are just as entitled to have them as everyone else is.

-Emily Maroutian

#201 – Lesson

When people ask me how I became so wise, I respond by saying, "Through years of being unwise." When they ask me how I'm so in balance with my emotions, I respond by saying, "Through years of imbalance." That's how you get there. Most people, however, don't want to admit their shortcomings. They don't want to face their faults. They don't want to look into their own depths and ask, "How can I grow from here?" They don't want to admit anything that might make them look bad in front of others. Most people already believe they know all they need to know and aren't open enough to get to a better place. Instead, they get by on habits. They resign into their current level of consciousness and choose not to self reflect.

-Emily Maroutian

#202 – Quote

Talking about the toxic past keeps it alive within us. Our
bodies respond to memories as if they are currently
happening. They can't tell the difference between recalling a
memory from long ago and real life. So reliving pain, trauma,
or suffering recreates the same experience in our bodies. We
make ourselves sick every time we retell an old story where we
feel the same anger or sadness again. One of the first steps to
healing is to reframe the past in a way that gives us power in
the present.

-Emily Maroutian

#203 – Advice

We are conditioned from a very young age to adopt everyone else's beliefs. At the age of 5, you don't get to choose what language you learn, what religion you are taught, which taboos your culture rejects, which stereotypes your parents pass on as truth, or which limitations you adopt from them. You are conditioned like this until you no longer need others to keep conditioning you. You do it automatically.

When someone challenges your conditioned truths, it makes you fearful or angry. You defend its existence because you believe it is reality. You argue for your limitations and feed your cycles because that is all you have ever known. To you, they are facts even if you don't like them, even if you wish they were different.

Other people's truths are different, but that doesn't necessarily make them bad. If you were born under different circumstances, you would believe a different truth. You might even believe what they believe. Stay open to others and what they have to offer. Just because they believe something different doesn't mean they are wrong.

-Emily Maroutian

#204 – Lesson

The concept of interconnectedness is described by many
different metaphors from various schools of thought. My
personal favorite one is called Indra's Net. Indra is a Vedic
God who created the universe as a giant web. At each vertex,
where the strings meet, there is a giant reflective jewel. Each
jewel reflects all the other jewels within the web. Like giant
mirrors, they hold each other's images within them. One
cannot be smudged, changed, cracked, or removed without
effecting all the others. This is a metaphor for the
interconnectedness of humanity. We cannot smudge
someone else's jewel without that being reflected within us as
well. What we do to others, we do to ourselves.

-Emily Maroutian

Forgiveness is only necessary when we don't recognize that we are the creators of our experiences. We only need to forgive after we have blamed. If we don't blame, we don't need to forgive. The people who help us create our experiences are only matches to our thinking. Forgiving them without shifting our internal conversations will only bring us more people to blame and then need to forgive.

-Emily Maroutian

#206 – Advice

If you spend most of your life and most of your energy trying to be lovable, you will make yourself so tired and so afraid of being yourself that you will never even be open to accepting real love. You will become so afraid of losing it that you will lose it over and over again. Let go of the need to be lovable for others and choose yourself. Let the love that comes to you be real, not just convenient and conditional for whoever is around you.

-Emily Maroutian

#207 – Lesson

When you accept that the only power you have is over yourself, when you wake up to the reality that there is a deep interconnectedness between everything, then you won't feel the need to control anyone but yourself. And in controlling yourself, you will control everything else as a result.

It's one of life's ironies. The more you try to control, the more everything is out of your control. When you stop trying to control others and just focus on yourself, you then begin to alter everything around you. It's in the release of power that we gain it.

-Emily Maroutian

Generation after generation, we raise individuals who are afraid of everything in the world. Afraid of their neighbors, afraid of strangers, afraid of animals, afraid of the food they eat, the water they drink, the air they breathe, their governments, their parents, their teachers, and even their God. We raise individuals who are afraid of life. They are afraid to live because maybe they might do something that will cause them to die. So they stop living, and they die anyway.

-Emily Maroutian

#209 – Advice

Sometimes, to protect your self-esteem or self-image, your mind might create negativity toward other people to cover up your insecurities. It will convince you of many false things about others to make you feel better about yourself.

Don't believe everything you think. Some things are just meant to ease you, not to be taken as fact. You can tell when this is occurring if you feel great pleasure in negatively thinking or talking about other people.

-Emily Maroutian

#210 – Lesson

We live in a fear-based society where most of our actions are motivated by our fear of loss or our fear of the unknown. The purchases we make, the way we live, the relationships we choose, the jobs we stay stuck in—most of what we do is based on a fear we are trying to subdue. We are afraid of stepping out into the unknown and taking a chance because our real fear is losing what we have already created.

Fear eventually turns into anger, which is meant to push us through the wall of fear and into action. It allows us the courage to act when we would normally be paralyzed by our fear. Years of feeling stuck with fear can lead to a burst of anger that finally allows us to shift something within our lives.

-Emily Maroutian

#211 – Quote

The type of life you have will depend on whether you fight *with* yourself or *for* yourself. If you spend most of your energy struggling with your own thoughts and emotions, then you won't have any left over for the obstacles on the path to your dreams. You'll give up easily because you'll be exhausted. You won't have any more fight in you because you will have inadvertently defeated yourself.

-Emily Maroutian

#212 – Advice

The first part of change happens within us. We begin to think and feel differently and therefore respond differently to everyday things. Soon after, the everyday things begin to change as a result of our responses. However, there is a period of time when the everyday things still look the same on the outside. Don't confuse that with failure. There's a creation delay when it comes to change. The external matches the internal bit-by-bit. It's never a complete change overnight.

There are pieces of the change throughout the day even if they're small in comparison to the changes within. It's enough to show us that it's working. They're like breadcrumbs showing you the path. It's important to pay close attention to them and acknowledge that it's working.

We have to keep going. If we change our energy back during this delay, it'll feel like nothing changed at all. We'll think we failed. So keep steady in your change and give it some time. The world has to adjust to your energy, and that happens bit-by-bit until one day you realize that everything is different.

-Emily Maroutian

#213 – Lesson

Most people don't see the pain or trauma they create for other people. They are so focused on trying to avoid the pain and trauma for themselves that they can't see what they're doing to the person in front of them. It is almost always unintentional.

The father who leaves does so because *he* feels like a failure. The boyfriend who cheats does so because *he* feels insecure. The mother who screams does so because *she* feels powerless.

People act out of their own need to avoid pain for themselves, and in doing so they cause pain to others. It's not intentional and it's not personal. People just don't know any other way of dealing with their emotions. They were never taught how, so they do the best they can in the moment. And sometimes, that means leaving or screaming or giving up.

-Emily Maroutian

#214 – Quote

Your body is a result of the life you have lived. If it's tired, sick, or overburdened with weight, it's a reflection of the thoughts and feelings that have affected it. When you shift your thinking, and therefore shift your feelings, your body will follow suit.

-Emily Maroutian

#215 – Advice

In times of deep darkness, even the tiniest of light makes a difference. It allows us to see the next step and the next until we can find our way out. We have to follow the light of hope, however small it may be, and wherever it may lead. Sometimes, the way out can be found in the unlikeliest of places. We simply need to follow the light.

-Emily Maroutian

#216 – Lesson

You are looking at where you are in your life with your current eyes, and that's why you're not moving forward. If you look at your current place with new eyes, they'll lead you to a new place. They'll notice all of the things you didn't see before because you were used to seeing them one way. You have to start seeing your life in a different way if you want to create a different life. Your new eyes will see the new possibilities and paths to the new horizons, and all you will have to do is follow it.

-Emily Maroutian

#217 – Quote

Pain is a result of emotional resistance. It shows up in the body after we've been fighting with our circumstances, lives, family members, and our own emotions for a while. Pain doesn't lie. It can't be denied or ignored. It demands our attention because it's trying to show us something. It's pointing the way to where we need healing internally. If we can be gentle with ourselves as we try to heal, then we are already halfway there. If we can find more relaxing and easy thoughts, then we can perpetuate our healing much faster because pain is a result, not a cause. If we can intentionally relax the cause, the result will ease as well.

-Emily Maroutian

#218 – Advice

Light and dark are mutually exclusive; they can't exist together in the same spot. One has to give into the other. Wherever you shine a light, it makes the darkness disappear. Light wins every time. Regardless of how deep and frightening the darkness is, it will always give into the light.

Take your light everywhere you go, and you will never need to fear what's in the dark unknown. As long as you're there, all will be well. The darkness can't have any power over you if you bring your own light.

-Emily Maroutian

#219 – Lesson

Evil is a mental concept born out of contrast. It is an idea, a judgment. We look at other people's behavior, and we judge it as good or evil based on what we were raised to believe. Even the most perceivably evil people believe that they are doing good when they battle against us. Entire wars are fought with each side believing that the other is evil and therefore needs to be defeated. Good and bad are matters of perspective.

No person is born into an evil/bad race or group. A "bad" mind is born out of a process of thoughts. And most of those thoughts justify their own existence through habit. All beliefs are understandable from their corresponding perspectives.

-Emily Maroutian

#220 – Quote

Compassion is our ability to see our own darkness in others and not judge them for it. Judgment and criticism is our refusal to see that we all share the same pain even if we come by it differently.

-Emily Maroutian

#221 – Advice

What you don't embrace in yourself, you will fear or hate in others. The feeling of disapproval is a self-reflective emotion. We reject parts of ourselves and condemn other people for mirroring it back to us.

Love yourself completely, and you won't find faults in other people. You'll be more understanding and less judgmental. You'll be more peaceful and less combative. You'll see deeper than you ever have, and it will inspire you to be kinder.

The faults we find in others are usually our own. When we accept ourselves for who we are, it makes it easier to accept others.

-Emily Maroutian

#222 – Quote

We believe that we can measure time, but we use ourselves as the measurement. Time is relative to us: our planet, spinning around our sun, in our galaxy. That is how we measure time. However, our galaxy holds fifty billion planets and five billion suns. Not only that, but there are hundreds of billions of galaxies in the visible universe. How many billions of suns and planets exist in those billions of galaxies? What is time for the universe?

-Emily Maroutian

#223 – Advice

Helping another person puts you in the position to learn how to help yourself. As you do things for other people, you discover new ways to do them for yourself as well. You benefit most of all because you learn and grow from your experiences with others.

Ask someone if you can help them with something new, something you've never tried before. They'll be grateful for the help, and you'll learn how to do something you've never done before. It's a win-win because when you serve others, you also serve yourself.

-Emily Maroutian

#224 – Lesson

All states of mind are just habits of thought. Repeating anxious thoughts creates an anxious mind that automatically reacts to the outside world through anxiety, regardless of what happens. As we practice it every day, it becomes easier and easier to respond in the same old way. Repeating angry thoughts or sad thoughts does the same. But so does repeating grateful thoughts and joyful thoughts. It's all just a matter of creating new habits of thought.

-Emily Maroutian

Artists that can't create might become destructive instead. If the overwhelming need to express isn't released in a healthy way, it'll force its way out through other means. Sometimes, they might act out, lose control of themselves, destroy their relationships, or hate their lives. They might stop caring about everything around them, and they might even turn against themselves, often exploding in fits of rage or sinking into a deep depression. One minute, their emotions may be high; the next minute, they may be low. Creative release is a balancer of emotions. When it's taken away, artists can show signs of mental illness. However, they're not sick; the energy is just exiting through a different door.

-Emily Maroutian

#226 – Advice

Make niceness the absolute minimum requirement in friends and significant others. Most people use that characteristic as the defining factor in choosing friendships and relationships when it should be the bare minimum.

Kindness should be higher on the list because being nice can be a mask for ulterior motives. Niceness can easily be faked for selfish reasons. People can be nice to you just to get something from you. Kindness, however, is much harder to fake and is usually more authentic.

-Emily Maroutian

#227 – Lesson

Muslims get their prayers answered just as often as Christians and Hindus do. If people did not experience some form of proof from their beliefs, they would stop believing in them. The universe is set up to support every single person through energy, vibration, and focused consciousness.

-Emily Maroutian

The relationship between the government and its people is similar to that of a child and parent. If the child behaves in an alarming or immoral way, it is the duty of the parent to step in and guide the child. It is the parent's right to question the behavior of the child and even correct unacceptable behavior.

Governments are created by the people and exist because of the people. And even though most see them as the parent in this situation, they are really the child. They are children pushing boundaries and seeing how far they can get away with reckless behavior. Your criticism of its actions is not unpatriotic; it's mandatory for healthy development. It is not only your right but your duty to raise a better government.

-Emily Maroutian

#229 – Advice

The easiest thing you can do in life is blame your parents for your own limitations and shortcomings as an adult. Don't go down that line of reasoning. It will be easy to do, but it won't get you anywhere in life. It won't help you overcome those limitations. It won't help you become stronger or wiser. It won't open doors for you, and it won't help you develop your talents or skills. It will just give you an easy out from trying anything meaningful. If you take the out, you won't expect much from yourself because you will use it as an excuse. If you believe you've been set up to fail, you won't even try to succeed.

-Emily Maroutian

#230 – Lesson

People will tell you a lot of things throughout your life. They'll tell you the right way to dress, the right way to act, to behave, to think, to feel, to believe. They'll tell you what to value and what to disregard. They'll tell you everything based on who they are and what works for them. Your parents, teachers, friends, co-workers—the whole world—will tell you who you should be and how you should be. One day, you'll realize that you don't have to be any of it and it's all your choice. That day will be the first day of *your* life.

-Emily Maroutian

Most people believe that they are not responsible for their actions as long as other people trigger them. If they are angered or provoked into action, then they feel justified in behaving negatively. They willingly allow others to have the power over their emotions because it excuses them from the responsibility of behaving appropriately. As long as someone else is seen as the cause, they feel vindicated in creating a negative effect.

We are responsible for our actions as well as our reactions. We don't get a pass because others behave in one particular way or another. Who we are is not defined by how others behave. Who we are is defined by how we behave.

-Emily Maroutian

#232 – Advice

People you don't like still have something valuable to offer
you. Just because you don't like them doesn't mean they're
not smart or talented or skilled. They've lived a life different
from yours, and their experiences have shaped them in their
own special way. They may see things differently from you,
but that doesn't mean they are wrong or bad. If you listen
with an open mind instead of waiting to dislike what they
have to say, you might learn something valuable. Don't wait to
be offended; expect to gain something of use from each
encounter.

-Emily Maroutian

#233 – Lesson

The difference between letting go and quitting is the difference between releasing your hold on something verses dropping it. When you let go, you allow that thing to be free. You release it with no sense of loss. When you quit, you abandon it and feel the emptiness of its space. Letting go gives you a sense of relief and freedom, while quitting gives you guilt, shame, or regret. Letting go brings you the feelings of wholeness and content, while quitting leaves you feeling like you lost something.

-Emily Maroutian

#234 – Quote

If you're anchored to the past by someone or something that won't let you move forward, eventually you will have to decide if you want to continue to stay there or cut the rope.

-Emily Maroutian

#235 – Advice

Choose yourself. Choose your problems, your faults, your pain, and all your suffering. Choose to love all that you are in all the ways that you are. Choose your family, your friends, your job, and everything you have. Choose this moment right here, right now. Resist nothing. Be in an everlasting state of acceptance of every moment that is, and you will transform your entire life.

-Emily Maroutian

#236 – Lesson

If you look back at your past self and feel completely justified in your choices, then you haven't grown much from who you used to be. If you look back with judgment and feel stupid about your past choices, then you have grown from who you used to be. But if you look back with love and understanding for who you were and why you needed to do what you did, then you have matured. Being an adult isn't about justification for or judgment of our past. It's about understanding and feeling love for who we were and what we did regardless of why we did it.

-Emily Maroutian

#237 – Quote

Who you are is a collection. A collection of stardust and minerals. A collection of bacteria and cells. A collection of matter and energy. A collection of memories and experiences. You are made of millions of "other" things that exist within this world and even outside of it. You can never be alone because you are not one; you are many.

-Emily Maroutian

#238 - Advice

Be yourself. The entire universe came together as it did for billions of years resulting in the one in four hundred trillion chance of your birth. There can only ever be one you, and it's here and now. It will never exist ever again. There is only one person who has and can ever have all of your memories, thoughts, emotions, and past experiences combined exactly as it is now. No one else can mimic that or have that. It's statistically and biologically impossible. You are special. Never ever forget that.

-Emily Maroutian

Thank you for reading the little droplets of wisdom I've discovered during my first thirty years. I've learned many lessons through multiple teachers and am grateful for each and every one of them. They have taught me directly and indirectly, through laughter and tears, through joy and pain. I hope some of them resonated with you. Feel free to highlight them, bookmark them, rip them out and put them up. Use them in anyway that benefits you or makes your life easier. They are my gift to you.

45714739R00150

Made in the USA
San Bernardino, CA
15 February 2017